AF618508

Benjamin Thiele

12

Spiritual Cosmology

The Essence of God, Karma, Astrology and Religions

© tao.de in Kamphausen Media GmbH, Bielefeld

1. Edition 2018

Author: Benjamin Thiele
Cover Design: Benjamin Thiele
Cover Photography: NASA
Language Assistant: Laura Mugford
Layout: Benjamin Thiele

Production: tredition GmbH, Halenreie 40-44, 22359 Hamburg

Publisher: tao.de in Kamphausen Media GmbH, Bielefeld,
www.tao.de, eMail: info@tao.de

ISBN Paperback: 978-3-96240-292-1
ISBN e-Book: 978-3-96240-293-8

Das Werk, einschließlich seiner Teile, ist urheberrechtlich geschützt. Jede Verwertung ist ohne Zustimmung des Verlages unzulässig. Dies gilt insbesondere für die elektronische oder sonstige Vervielfältigung, Übersetzung, Verbreitung und sonstige Veröffentlichung

Table of Contents

Preface

Starting from the original motivation to improve my practice as a karmic astrologist and regression therapist by gaining a deeper understanding of the astrologic house system, there was an unexpected and intense exchange with a source of inspiration over a two week period in April 2018.

This exchange led to me writing this book. It has no other objective than to bring clarity about the identity of God and human beings in a confused world full of different religions, philosophies and ideals.

This clarity leads to a view of the world and to a spiritual framework which is non-religious but still includes many proven beliefs and practices of traditional religions.

I understand religions as partially valuable and partially clumsy attempts of the young, developing mankind to approach the big questions about our identity as human beings.

Irrespective from the fact that many people distance themselves from religions due to their growing self-confidence and personal convictions, a society should not distance itself from the big questions themselves. Mankind should, in fact, always keep searching for answers.

Of course, this search for answers will not be over in the foreseeable future. At this stage, nothing in this book or in any other book can provide a perfect answer. Yet according to the degree of understanding of how the universe was created, a new, non-religious and loving spiritual framework also has space to grow and positively influence all aspects of life. This will lead to harmonic relationships between humans, nature and the spiritual realm, also known as the subtle world, which constantly surrounds us. And this evolutionary step will happen because of conviction and not as a result of tradition or enforcement.

1. The 12 Fields – The Path of the Universe

Everything that is born has to perish. This very fundamental concept is valid for the human body, our planet and eventually the whole universe itself.
Creation is always cyclic and goes straight back to its origin. The symbol of a cyclic process is the circle.
For all readers that are familiar with astrology, the cycle of the 12 Fields will purposely start at '12.' This will make it easier to understand the astonishing analogy with modern astrology later on.

Field 12

Before creation, the universe was in a state beyond creation. This state is unexplainable, highly mystical and cannot be realised cognitively.

Our very limited language capabilities and our way of thinking as human beings on earth evolved historically through interaction between the mortal and polarity-bound humans with other human beings and the surrounding environment. Therefore, our language and way of thinking work in terms of space, time, daily routine, human relations and relations with the environment.
All of these aspects are very limited experiences within the creation spectrum, but are not appropriate for putting the state beyond creation into words.
Furthermore, compared with the universe, mankind is extremely small, young and naïve. This is another obstacle standing in the way of answering the very big questions of life.

An artist can reflect on his painting, but the painting cannot reflect on the artist.
All attempts to describe the state beyond creation fundamentally lead to at least partially wrong answers.
'God' is a widely used name for this state, or infinity. In Yoga philosophy, it is called 'Sat-Chit-Ananda,' meaning 'infinite power, infinite knowledge and infinite bliss.' This is an interesting attempt to assign at least some characteristics to the state of infinity, which is actually beyond being able to be characterised.
Due to various historic and partially even pictorial associations with 'God,' this name has become biased. It often proposes that God is a higher being that watches over us.
God is not a person but a historic name for this un-explainable state of infinity.
The best and most faultless definition may come from an Indian spiritual teacher, who simply said: "It is what it is."

If the truth-seeking and curious mind wants to at least get closer to understanding this state beyond creation, the easiest way would be to explain what it is not:
This state is beyond everything that can be perceived i.e. beyond space, time, energy, matter, consciousness and all other forms of polarity and connections to creation.
In this spiritual state, absolutely nothing exists, but there is the potential for everything imaginable to exist: anything and everything is possible. Furthermore, any creation - however complex it may be - could be manifested without any effort, since infinity is – by definition - not limited by any laws or restrictions.
If there was a rule limiting infinity, infinity would no longer be infinite. And if there was still such a restriction, where

did it originate from? Any phenomenon has a beginning, an end, a cause and a creator.
So was creation a mood? Was it done out of boredom? Was it a shock towards realising one's own existence? Was it a desire for diversity? Was it a wake-up call? Is all of this simply a game?
Strictly speaking, creation is none of these, but we don't know which idea comes closest. Nevertheless, this nebulosity is not a big issue because our challenges as human beings are still far away from answering this particular question.

Field 1

Within the infinite and passive state (12), a dynamic suddenly appears. Within the cycle of the 12 Fields, this step is maybe the most mysterious and important one. A first movement occurs, which originates from infinity but leaves infinity itself unchanged.
Within infinity, a mighty yet limited sense of will arises, which spreads in all directions in an unobstructed way. This impulse carries the intent, power and the plan for creation (House 1, Aries).

Before creation came about, this impulse of will did not exist. It originated from infinity but it is not infinite itself. Therefore, it is descriptive yet a little provocative to call the resulting creation a mere thought; a divine dream; a divine shadow or a divine illusion.
Creation is real because it happens. It is real because we can perceive it at every moment. Yet it is simultaneously

not real because it does not hold the nature of infinity: it will one day disappear.

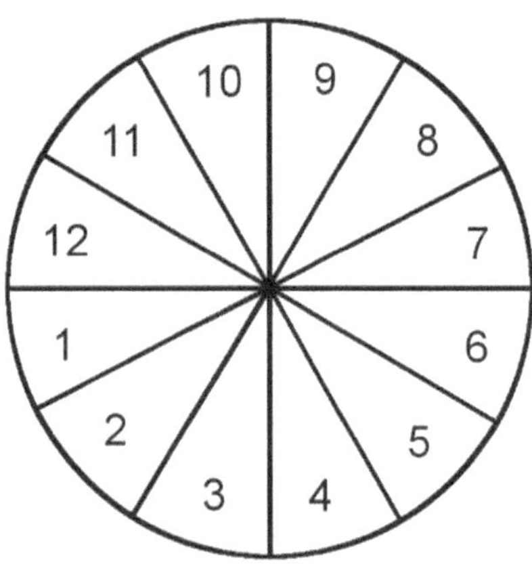

Image 1: The cycle of the 12 Fields

As a result of this impulse of will, a phenomenal world would be created. In physics, this would be referred to as the singularity of the 'Big Bang,' which happened around 15 billion years ago. This was the moment in which space, time, energy, matter and laws of nature were created and began to interact with one another.

A universe would be painted like a picture, but so far there is only one colour; namely the divine light itself. And this colour is everywhere in the same, infinite intensity, since everything is one and neither space nor time exist.
It is now the divine 'trick' to create space and time (canvas) in order to carry the painting later on.

Field 2

The interaction between light and the absence of light creates different kinds of energies, energy clouds, atoms and aggregations of matter (House 2, Taurus).

The architecture of the atom reveals how diversity is created, namely through the combination of light (particles) and the absence of light (empty space, darkness), as already mentioned. These components and their various combinations result in an apparent substantial diversity, although the nature of infinity is an inseparable unity.
Yet as infinity – by definition – contains everything, it must also contain the absence of anything: nothingness.

The infinity that became active during creation still exists, unchanged, but it is now surrounded by seemingly external objects that can be perceived and controlled.
Therefore, within the all-encompassing infinity, there is now a subject (ego, centre of consciousness) and an object (the objects of creation within time and space).
Infinity is the creator of these objects: its light is the substance of these objects and its light pervades the entire universe. This is why some mystics call creation the 'shadow of God.'

Field 3

In this stage, a primitive consciousness evolves that can perceive the created objects and reflect on them. This perception is only possible because there is a connection to the objects.

In the next step, attributes such as "small"/"big" can be given to these objects by the consciousness.
This cognitive mode of operation is called 'judgement,' which can only occur through 'perception' (House 3, Gemini).

Field 4

Conscious perception and the subdivision of objects gradually leads to habits of thinking and to the rise of emotions. Sympathy, antipathy, joy, satisfaction and so on arise within the consciousness towards the perceived objects.
The consciousness holds on to whatever is perceived or classified as beautiful. Aesthetically displeasing objects are avoided (House 4, Cancer).
Instead of always realising the true identity of infinity, the ego starts to feel attracted to something that is created and endless by nature.
Desire and passion arise. This also leads to karma. Consciousness (3) comes from God (12) and possesses a creative force and willpower (1) respectively. Every desire that arises in this consciousness must be fulfilled somehow, sooner or later, and everything that still needs to be fulfilled contributes directly to karma.

Field 5

The consciousness follows the steadily growing urge for the desired objects. This can even mean uniting with such objects: the ego wants to feel satisfaction by being

surrounded with these objects or by uniting with them (House 5, Leo).
We can compare this to looking at a beautiful landscape on a photograph. Looking at it can spark a desire to travel to this place, and this desire goes beyond judgement (3) and emotions (4). In fact, it means 'passion.'

The Fields (1) to (4) lead to an ego because there is now a centre of perception and outer objects that can apparently be perceived by the ego. As passion grows, the ego becomes fully evolved. Yet as the ego steadily interacts with the created objects around it, infinity itself gets involved, or, rather, is entrapped in its own creation. This then leads to a growing and voluntary bonding to lower energies and eventually matter, being the lowest form of energy.
To be God itself is the true identity of consciousness, but this idea gets lost within the low frequencies of matter. Instead, a steadily growing identification with the perceived and desired objects develops.

Field 6

In principle, the identification of consciousness goes through all states, from a gas state to solid stones to more and more complex and conscious creatures. For our purpose, it is sufficient to look at the last stage: identification with the human body (House 6, Virgo).
In the cycle of the 12 Fields, the sixth step lays opposite the initial infinite and passive state of the divine (12). Therefore, it must be the place where the dynamic state of God is at its peak and furthest away from its origin.

The dynamic of creation in the steps from (1) to (6) stops here. The swing of the pendulum has reached its maximum. Now, it can start to swing back to its origin via the Fields (7) to (12).

Despite, and because of, its infinity, consciousness brought itself into a position where it perceives itself as a very limited, mortal and unknowing object within creation.
Life on earth contains partially hostile conditions such as wild animals, diseases, natural disasters, hunger and so on. These conditions allow the divine consciousness to feel fear. It believes itself to be a mortal human being rather than identifying itself with infinity. This identification as a human being is a result of a lack of knowledge, or a kind of divine mistake, i.e. it is simply a wrong way of thinking. However, due to the divine power of will (1), this way of thinking is constantly energised, manifested and eventually becomes reality.

Whenever self-perception is faulty, there is a huge risk that, based on this mistake, further wrong conclusions will be made. And again, due to the power of will (1), these conclusions will also be manifested.
By living this way as a human being, a wide range of desires and dependencies arise, including sadness and anger when a desire is left unfulfilled.

Starting from the true nature of existence, 'Sat-Chit-Ananda,' which is infinite power, infinite knowledge and infinite bliss, infinity ends up on this level of existence (6) by having only limited power, lack of knowledge and conditional joy. The bliss of infinity disappears. Only very limited and temporary joy is left which can be perceived

by the body and its senses. And this limited joy which appears whenever desires are fulfilled often changes with suffering.
This gives us a better understanding of why human beings long for power, money and sensual pleasures of all kinds: these desires are simply sublimations for the lost 'paradise.' And since the incarnated human being cannot simply re-connect with divine bliss, these sensual pleasures seem to be unavoidable and therefore excusable.

Field 7

Despite this issue, it was never intended for infinity to get eternally entrapped into matter for the purpose of suffering and losing its true identity.
In this respect, a complex system consisting of loving beings was simultaneously installed to help us to return, enriched with experiences and wisdom by the steps (7) to (12), to our source and to our true identity.
Like ourselves, the beings that surround us are divine (12) but they have never been involved with matter. They still know who they are and their actions are based on knowledge rather than the absence of knowledge.

By getting entrapped in a human body, the divine consciousness makes the experience of interpersonal relationships for the very first time (House 7, Libra). This is a new experience since the divine consciousness is, in fact, one and everything. It therefore cannot interact.
This achievement of interaction is also one of the biggest challenges of being human.

The immense range of interpersonal relationships leads to many painful and unbalanced actions, and so karma is increased. The cycle of re-incarnation becomes necessary. We can only get rid of karma where it began. This is why we go through a wide range of interpersonal relationships, reaching from domination to being dominated, from affection to aversion, from love to hate, from cooperation to intrigues, and from war to peace.

Field 8

Through re-incarnation, the consciousness that is entrapped in creation is confronted with events in an appropriate intensity and space of time. And this composition reflects and corrects all biased and unbalanced desires and actions.
This cyclic and emotionally intense process means 'transformation' (House 8, Scorpio).
Transformation, as such, is related to the principle of life and death. Something wrong, such as the identification as a human being, needs to die in order to give way for the truth (birth).

In this manner, the soul goes through a huge range of intensive experiences (health, disease, wealth, poverty etc.), all of which are composed and shared out according to the individual evolutionary needs and the karma of the embodied soul.
Irrespective of the level of pain associated with these experiences, there is a loving plan behind this, and an invisible hand that guides us into and through these experiences is always present.

Field 9

This composed process leads to a steady growth (House 9, Sagittarius) of self-awareness and unconditional love. Some may also call this 'wisdom.' Within the circle of the 12 Fields, it is not a coincidence that this field lays directly opposite field (3).

Both fields build the axis of the mind, consisting of the two functions 'intellect' and 'wisdom.' Even though all 12 fields within the cycle are equally important, this axis is somewhat special. In several ways, it is the heart of the cycle and the middle between the original state of God (12) and the apparent human being (6).

Both axes form a rectangular cross: they are the backbone of the whole cycle.

Father/Creator (12), son/object (6) and the holy ghost (3,9).

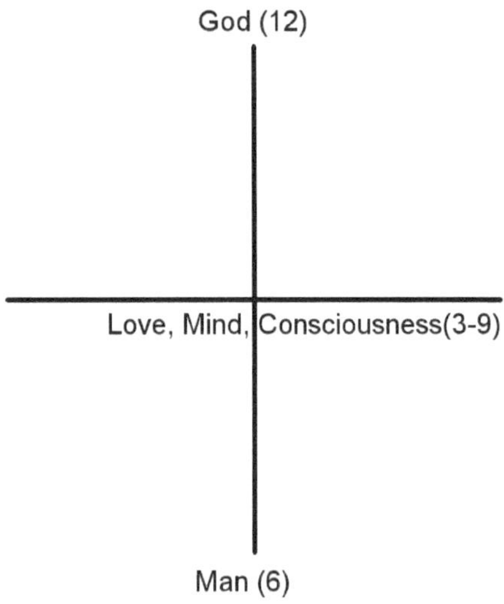

Image 2: The backbone of the 12 Fields

Love keeps everything together. Without it, as a motivation and harvest, the universe could remain in stage (12) or would not return from stage (6). It is the centre of the movement of the pendulum between (12) and (6).

Field 10

Provided the degree of self-awareness and love are deep enough and karma is erased, self-realisation can happen (House 10, Capricorn). The human being that had until now been bound to karma now realises that it had always been divine in its essence, and always will be.

Depending on the cultural background, such a person could be called a saint, a self-realised soul, a spiritual master or an enlightened being.
These beings have a deeper understanding that although actions can be taken, it is only God that can act through everything and everybody.
Despite this increased level of consciousness and understanding, saints still have an ego and individual character. The brain and sub-consciousness are still programmed and contain affections that do not just suddenly disappear. Saints react when their name is called; they still possess a body and a character, symbolising the echo of their past lives.
This soul is now liberated from the cycle of re-incarnation but it is still not God in its infinite, omnipotent and almighty state (12).

Field 11

During the next stage, the enlightened being can continue to get rid of its remaining ego. This steadily leads to a harmonic merging with the whole of creation (House 11, Aquarius).

Field 12

When creation itself comes to rest, the whole cycle of the universe ends in the endless and peaceful state of Field 12, where the whole movement had once began.

On its mysterious path from (12) to (6), the universe voluntarily became involved in its own creation. In favour of a learning process, it accepted that pain and confusion are things that can be experienced. The closer it got to (6), the lower the frequency became and the less the consciousness remembered that it is actually (12) itself.

Souls, apparently individual and independent beings, existed on this path because infinity looked at its creation through many eyes simultaneously.
These souls existed over thousands of years, and in this respect it is understandable and acceptable to grant them their own kind of existence. However, strictly speaking, there are no souls because everything originates from the unity displayed in Field (12). And this is true for every object, every soul, every condition and even for space and time as a mere temporary framework for creation.
None of the 12 fields are wrong or worthless. The whole thing is a cyclic movement and will definitely return to its origin before a new cycle can be started, and no soul will ever get lost during this journey.

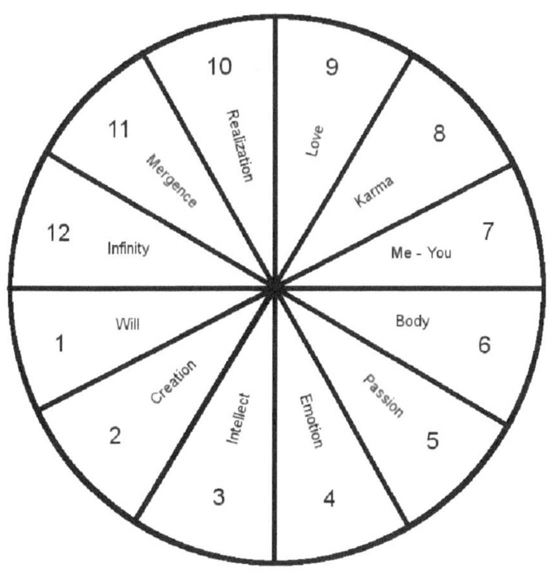

Image 3: The labeled circle of the 12 Fields

2. The Equivalence of the 12 Fields in the Human Being

According to the bible, man is created in God's image. This can be interpreted in many ways but it fits nicely into the 12 Fields:

1) Chakras: On an energetic and subtle level, there are centres of energy within us - so called chakras. They work like organs and have individual functions and aspects. They are funnel-shaped energetic swirls whose functions can be directly perceived through emotions and physical symptoms of the body. The most important 7 chakras along the human backbone have 12 openings to our environment that correspond to the 12 Fields.

2) Psychology: the human psychology contains all 12 Fields at once. Their individual combination, accentuation and intensity make up the unique character of man, and this individual combination can be analysed, for example, through astrology.

Chakras

To this date, the energetic aspects behind the chakras are sufficiently but not yet fully known. One reason is due to a lack of consistent records from beings who have experienced a full opening of one chakra or even several chakras.
Consequently, chakra-related literature contains descriptions that are sometimes ambiguous or vague.

There has been more sufficient research into which physical and organic areas are affected in the case of a chakra malfunction.

The highest chakra is called crown chakra. It is located in the crown of the head and opens vertically into the divine consciousness (12).

The third-eye chakra is located below this in the middle of the head. It has one opening on the forehead (11) and one at the back of the head (1). An open third eye leads to willpower (1) and the whole universe can be seen at once (11).

The throat chakra is in the middle of the neck and has one ventral opening (10) and one dorsal (2). A fully open throat chakra enables the realisation and manifestation of matter and energy (2).

The heart chakra is located near the physical heart and has a ventral opening on the chest (9) and a dorsal one (3) on the back. The axis (3, 9) is the centre of the divine world (12) and the physical world, symbolised by the body (6). It is associated with the consciousness, i.e. the mind, which reflects on the world intellectually (3) and holistically (9). Intellect is the little brother of wisdom, and intellect alone cannot grasp the universe in its entirety. It easily gets lost in flawed psychological concepts and misinterpretations. Having said that, pure wisdom does not provide the strategic way of thinking needed in order to organise and complete pragmatic tasks in this world.

The solar plexus is located near the navel and has a ventral opening (8) and a dorsal one (4). This is where the subconscious is located. All emotions (4) within the current incarnation and all previous ones (8) are stored here. By the application of suitable techniques, these memories can be selectively recalled. Psychological subjects such as 'the inner child' or 'past life regressions' take place here.

The sacral chakra is located below the navel and has a ventral (7) and dorsal (5) opening. It stands for sexuality, which is composed of the passionate urges (5) of an individual to unite with another individual (7). Therefore, the sacral chakra embodies aspects of creativity, physical creativity (children), joy of living and the relationships to other people in general.

The root chakra is located at the lower end of the spine and opens vertically towards the earth (6). It stands for the will to survive or for life force. These are fundamental aspects of the embodied individual (6) in a partially hostile environment on planet earth (or on any other planet).

In order to fully activate a chakra, it requires the activation of the corresponding fields along the axis of reflection between (6) and (12).

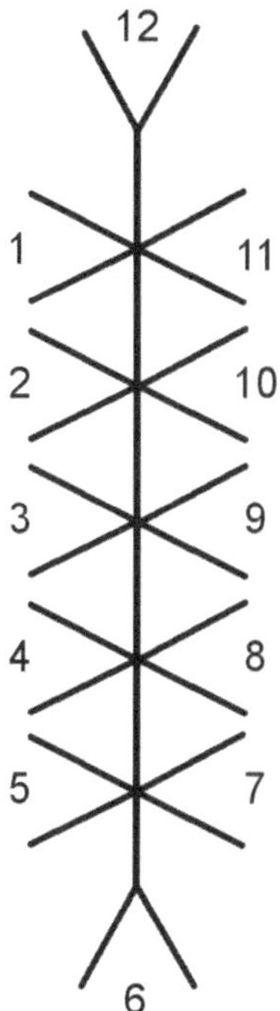

Image 4: The 7 chakras and the 12 Fields along the vertical backbone (axis 6, 12)

Fields (6) and (12) can be opened directly. Field (6) connects to the earth while field (12) connects to infinity.

The sacral chakra can be opened fully when a complete sexual fusion (5) with another person (7) occurs.

The solar plexus opens fully when the subconscious emotions (4) and karma (8) are successfully solved and no negative emotions remain.

The heart chakra opens fully whenever intellect (3) and wisdom (9) are fully evolved and work hand in hand as a loving and knowing mind.

The throat chakra opens fully when the human being becomes one with the surrounding energies and matter.

The third eye opens fully when the individual will (1) becomes one with the whole universe (11) and the cosmic will respectively.

Each of these hypothetical openings is based on the principle of union, and this can - in other words - be interpreted as love. However, this does not mean the kind of love experienced in a partnership or any other kind of desiring love, but love in the spiritual sense of being unconditional, all-encompassing and harmonic.

In this early evolutionary stage of mankind, it is very rare for a chakra to be fully open. Typically, the chakras are only slightly active and only slightly open. This leads to less powerful abilities in daily life:

A slightly open crown chakra opens the way for higher energies and inspiration.

A slightly open third eye leads to intuition, willpower and clairvoyance.

A slightly open throat chakra leads to connectivity and harmonic communication with the surrounding environment.

A slightly open heart chakra opens the mind and leads to a state of happiness.

A slightly open solar plexus strengthens self-confidence.

A slightly open sacral chakra promotes sexuality, joy of living and the connection to other people.

A slightly open root chakra activates physical energy and strengthens the will to live.

The energy flow between the chakras corresponds to the path of the universe in the 12 Fields. You can find an energy flow from top to bottom (12, 1, 2, 3, 4 ...) and from bottom to top (6, 7, 8, 9, etc.).

In general, the energy in our energetic system comes from above (12). This energy then goes down through the main energetic channel (spine) and back up from the root chakra (6) through a parallel energetic channel.
In an energetically unhealthy or unbalanced person, this flow can be partially blocked because a chakra is not working properly. This could also negatively affect adjacent chakras. However, knowing this, chakras and energy flows can of course also be used to heal blockades e.g. by purposely transporting energy to them.

Psychology

It is one of the most important understandings that the individual human is of divine origin and of divine nature (12). It is God (12) in motion but it simply lost this knowledge and identification temporarily.

As being part of God and as being a kind of image of God, the human being does not possess infinite powers as they exist in (12). Humans are limited in terms of their knowledge, size and power.
A human being still possesses a limited willpower (1) and can collect/move/deform energy and matter (2).
We possess a mind that allows us to reflect and perceive intellectually (3) and holistically (9) in order to understand ourselves and our environment. Yet through the educated overemphasis of the intellectual thinking in the modern western hemisphere, the access to wisdom is impeded so that the essential connection between human (6) and God (12) is blocked.
By primarily using intellect, we build up mental concepts and views of the world that may seem plausible to us but that can be fundamentally wrong. To this date, human history is full examples of this.

All the emotions (4) of all incarnations (8) are stored in the subconscious and build our individual character. Approximately 80% of our activities and decisions are a result of this subconscious 'thinking,' although it is simply a container of good and bad memories.

There is a more or less strong urge within us to express ourselves egocentrically in the world (5) and to build relationships (7). Humans have goals in life and want to

achieve them (10) - no matter whether these goals are spiritual or worldly.
Sometimes consciously, but always subconsciously, humans possess an inner urge to unite with society and to become part of the whole world (11). It is not in our nature to be competing and isolated individuals, although some karmic traumas may indeed make some people temporarily prefer this concept in order to feel safe and protected.

It may gradually become clear that the individual - a created object within creation - goes through the cycle of the 12 Fields and carries these fields internally. Yet the interpretation of the 12 Fields is more pragmatic, limited, and refers to life on earth.
We need to look at the 12 Fields one octave lower and keep in mind that the limited human being is situated on earth as part of a re-incarnation cycle.

We can also derive from the 12 Fields that there are two competing forces within humans at any time: one force drags us into creation (1-6) whereas the other force drags us back to infinity (7-12). Both forces are always there, be it consciously or subconsciously. In former times, this was called temptation and salvation, or sometimes Brahma and Shiva, or even the devil and God. Yet in reality, these 12 Fields present a system to us that is harmonic and entirely made by God.

Even if we hypothetically assume for a moment that our existence in the world came about by a cosmic disaster, this would not actually change how we look at life and how we wish to master it.

Historically, many religions have repeatedly made the mistake of suggesting that people are guilty and sinners. This psychological concept is neither helpful nor justified. Simply because man is incarnated (8) and on its way back to infinity (12) does not mean that the steps (fields) previously taken were a mistake. Even if they were a mistake (hypothetically), it would be God's mistake and not the mistake of any human being born 15 billion years after creation.

Energetic Balance

The imbalance between the 12 Fields within the human mind can be seen as one possible cause for psychological, emotional and physical diseases. Therefore, it is not only beneficial for mastering the cycle of re-incarnation but also for becoming healthy, striving for a balance, and avoiding extremes.

A wild animal or a poison could directly harm the human body. This would obviously be a cause from (6) or (7).

Imbalance emerges when opposite fields are not lived out in a balanced way, for example when a human lives very passionately (5) without considering the needs of society (11).

Therefore, standardised rules and prohibitions can be individually inappropriate and harmful. Take a look at somebody who is over-sexualised: for this person, it can be beneficial to live abstinently for a limited period of time. By doing this, that person might be able to reduce their sexual energy to a normal level. A general prohibition of sexuality, celibacy, or a social taboo to suppress sexuality, very often has a negative effect. It can, in the worst case, lead to perversion or to aggressive sublimation.

A human that is too egocentric and strong willed (overemphasis of (1)) requires more focus on other people (polarity point of (1): (7)).

A human that holds onto material objects (overemphasis of (2)) requires a greater sense of the transience of existence (polarity point of (2): (8)).

A human that is too intellectual/cognitive (overemphasis of (3)) needs to open the mind for wisdom and love (polarity point of (3): (9)).

A human that is too emotional and adherent (overemphasis of (4)) needs to open for life and to become goal-oriented in order to achieve something (polarity point of (4): (10)).

A human that is impulsive (overemphasis of (5)) requires more consideration for the needs of society (11) and should try to find a productive role within society (polarity point of (5): (11)).

A human that is overly associated with his own body and life on earth (overemphasis of (6)) requires more focus on the divine world (polarity point of (6): (12)).

A human that is dependent from others (overemphasis of (7)) needs more self-confidence and individuality (polarity point of (7): (1)).

A human that lives in a constant state of change and tumult (overemphasis of (8)) requires more stability and to hold onto something (polarity point of (8): (2)).

A human that gets lost in holistic views (overemphasis of (9)) needs more cognitive structure and clarity (polarity point of (9): (3)).

A human that is goal-oriented and ambitious (overemphasis of (10)) requires more connection to emotional needs (polarity point of (10): (4)).

A human that is overly oriented on values of society (overemphasis of (11)) requires more urge and individuality (polarity point of (11): (5)).

A human that is over-spiritualised (overemphasis of (12)) requires more grounding and reference to the body (polarity point of (12): (6)).

Among the chakras, there are relations which have been researched already, and the polarities just mentioned confirm those relations. For example, in Reiki, there is a technique used to balance two chakras. This leads, coincidentally or not, to a structure much like the Jewish Menora (Image 5):

The root chakra (6) balances out with the crown chakra (polarity point of (6): (12)).

The third eye (1, 11) balances out with the sacral chakra (5, 7).

The throat chakra (2, 10) balances out with the solar plexus (4, 8).

The heart chakra (3, 9) does not balance out: it is the centre of the energetic system.

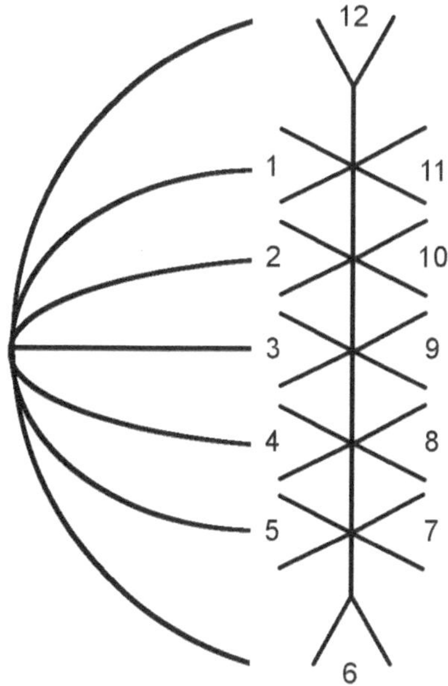

Image 5: Balancing the chakras

Resulting from the psychological aspects of the chakras and the energy flow between them, there are many ways to use our limited mind power creatively and heal ourselves.

Initially, the mind should be centered and calm, e.g. by focusing on the heart chakra. To achieve this, the Buddhist approach may be helpful, whereby breathing is observed because the lungs have a strong relationship with the heart chakra.

Then, we visualise a connection with the universe and the divine world 'above' via the crown chakra. We then establish a connection with the earth (6) so that old energies can leave our energetic system downwards.

Now, we use our sense of will (1) to protect ourselves during the session so that only positive energy can reach us (like a firewall).

The down-coming energy is high and omnidirectional. In the third eye, this energy gets a clear intent and 'stamping,' for example the cure of a fear or the increase of self-confidence. Then, we can guide this stamped energy along the backbone to its destination. In this example, the destination would be the solar plexus because it contains our emotions and fears. It may be beneficial to visualise old mental concepts leaving our energetic system forever via the root chakra.

Thanks to our (limited) willpower, this picture can now work automatically. In the case of mental digression, some of these steps can be repeated in order to softly push and maintain the energy flow from time to time.

This technique - one amongst many - can be felt by people that are familiar with energetic techniques. Yet every human being only possesses limited willpower and does not have the infinite will-power of God in Field (12).

Mind power exists as a matter of fact but its consequences are very limited. In esotericism, there are popular publications that suggest nearly endless possibilities to fascinated readers, claiming that the mind can achieve everything. This is simply not true and unintentionally misleading. The possession of nearly infinite powers in our confused state as human beings would be fatal for us, mankind and the whole universe.

The application of energetic techniques, visualisations, prayers, shamanic rituals, spiritual rituals, hypnoses etc. is, in principle, very valuable, but they require - depending on the individual case - being repeated and can even fail depending on the depth and intensity of the karma involved. Every single soul will one day be healed from all diseases and imbalances, but this process requires time and can only be supported and shortened.

3. The Architecture of the Spiritual Realm (Subtle World)

Every human being possesses a more or less evolved and trained intuition that can lead to experiences with the surrounding spiritual realm, also known as the subtle world or non-physical realm. When the soul leaves the body in the moment of physical death, it returns to this world in order to stay there for (normally) some years. This level of existence is, in comparison to life on earth, quite pleasant and easy. Many problems we face on earth do not exist there, or only to a degree that can be easily managed.
When we are born again, we receive a new brain and purposely temporarily forget about this level of existence in order to play our role on the stage of terrestrial life.

Yet, fortunately, there are many methods of getting an insight into this subtle world whilst being incarnated on earth. These methods are all based on the approach that the thinking mind (intellect) and emotions are calmed down in order to become receptive for the finer impressions and vibrations of the subtle world. These energies are always around and inside us; we just need to learn to switch off our minds in order to perceive them.

Very few people have the ability, through several opened chakras, to get in touch with non-physical realms at any time. Yet it is more common to live out these experiences under hypnosis (trance) or during meditation, as a result of shamanic rituals and many more.

People of all religions and times have had 'supernatural' experiences of some sort by applying some sort of traditional technique. In the bible, some main figures had contact with angels or maybe even God himself. The Koran has been passed by an archangel. American Indians, Siberians and others have applied shamanic rituals to get in touch with nature and their ancestors.

Unfortunately, many people who made such super-natural experiences concluded that their own belief system or religion must be superior because it led to such fascinating experiences. Yet every human being actually has the potential (energetic organs) to perceive the subtle world. In many cases, this ability is just not trained and therefore neglected.

The examination of all experiences man has ever made with the subtle world leads to a consistent understanding of the higher realms.

These realms are busy and occupied with disembodied souls which are - thanks to their perspective - much more knowledgeable than we are.
On this level, the advanced souls - and not the souls which are greedy for power- have all the power because the degree of evolution can directly be perceived by anybody.
Incarnated souls on earth are invisibly guided by those disembodied beings. The deceased get accompanied and cared for after they have left their body. The topics of the next incarnations get planned and discussed.
Past lives get analysed and also discussed, and
there are boards that steer the future of the whole planet.
Of course, there is a hierarchy in that world which corresponds to the evolutionary progress and its attained capabilities.

Beyond that, there are also loving beings that are directly sent from (12). They have never been incarnated before but they support the whole process invisibly. Those beings could be called 'angels' and their superiors are called 'archangels,' and this continues further.

In former times, humans were so awestruck that they thought any highly advanced soul that was perceived was God himself. In fact, those souls and angels deserve our gratitude and respect but they are simply part of what could be described as a huge company around planet earth consisting of officers, team leaders and senior management. And each disembodied being contributes according to its talents and evolutionary intents.
One department is responsible for watching over incarnated souls. The protective spirits working in this department care for individuals, houses, countries, companies and so on. Our world would be much more chaotic and destructive if responsibility was completely left to human beings.

In the subtle world, there are also beings that manage knowledge databases. During a regression, these door keepers unlock relevant past life memories that can be looked at by a therapist and the client. The therapist himself is only human and cannot know or decide which memories to look at from his limited perspective.
The fact that we normally cannot remember past lives is not a mistake but made on purpose. Yet in some cases, it is permitted and even required, especially when the client should leave his (cognitive) belief system and/or needs the healing of an old trauma.

Whenever a soul leaves the body in the moment of death, this point in time has already been known and planned within the subtle word.
In this emotionally challenging moment in which death is suddenly realised, the deceased is picked up by familiar and loved ones. They can then go back to the subtle world together through an energy channel within the next few days.
Unfortunately, we live in times where dying people can be so mentally confused and powerless that they do not acknowledge this channel. This leaves them irritated in an intermediate state between earth and the subtle world. Later on, when they become clearer and stronger, e.g. through prayers or places of power, they finally become aware of this channel and leave for the subtle world.
Whenever such beings become noticeable, they have been referred to as 'ghosts.'

Such a confused state may have many causes; it could result from a very energy-sapping medical therapy or severe alcoholism before the end of life. Since everything in the universe is connected, physical aspects clearly have an influence on the energetic system.

Even though the subtle world is enlightening and beautiful, life on earth can be challenging and painful to such an extent that souls temporarily turn into a state of hatred and complete confusion: they develop a 'bad' energy. They might then turn away from or even turn against the subtle world. Such destructive souls could be temporarily expelled from the community. There was a time when such souls would be referred to as 'demons.'
Eventually, they will continue their evolutionary path and find their way back to understanding and love, but this

sort of hatred and desperation could, in principle, develop in young and even mature souls. The backed-up negatives must discharge to give way for the light. This is, in fact, a transformation, and the enlightened beings can observe us in a level-headed way because they are well aware about this background. The saints of today are the mass murderers of yesterday.

Many people going through a tragedy wonder why God let it happen. Well, God in its original passive state (12) probably does not even consciously know that we exist right now. Yet God in its dynamic state (1, 2, 3, etc.) consists of beings that are loving but not almighty (12). Those are the ones we can reach through prayers, but they can only react according to our karma, scheme of life and our evolutionary intent. Since we normally do not know much about these intents, strokes of fate leave us confused and insecure.

4. Historic Spiritual Parallels

The knowledge about the 12 Fields can be found in many traditional philosophies:

Jesus

The bible contains precious spiritual wisdom originating from highly advanced souls. The questionable and incomplete documentation and communication of knowledge leaves us with a book that is, compared to its simple message, very voluminous, imperfect and decoded. The essence is subject to research and interpretation, but research and interpretation give room to misinterpretation.
Interestingly, Genesis, which is wrong from a scientific point of view, also ends up with the creation of man (6, Adam) on the sixth step (day). Then, interpersonal relationships are made possible by God through the creation of Eve (7). The fall of mankind binds man to life and death (8) with the long-term objective to find the way back to God (9, 10, 11, 12).

Cain and Abel also fit in nicely to Field (8). After the vertical fall of mankind, one man acts for the first time against another man. This is the horizontal fall of mankind through a lack of love, wisdom and understanding. This further increases karma (8) and binds man to the world.
In the sense of the bible, this is divine punishment. However, I look at this as karma, which requires balancing and clearing.

According to the 12 Fields, it is a state of every soul to be God's son because everything originates from (12) and everything that exists is God in motion.
God moves in mysterious ways. The origin (12) is incomprehensible. Nobody should try to make any image of God; not because God might get angry, but because it is simply not possible. God in motion can be seen every moment, but God in its state of infinity (12) is not an object that could ever be perceived. It is, in fact, the origin of objects.

Through the frequency of incarnation, souls reach a certain degree of wisdom. In all regions at all points in time, advanced souls have been leaving the cycle of re-incarnation or were just about to leave it.
Sometimes, they voluntarily return to earth for charity's sake: some of them belong to religions; some practise outside religions; some practise publically; some in secrecy. One of these public souls was Jesus.

In a relatively dark time where the karma of mankind deteriorated to a critical degree, Jesus shared his deep understandings of life and taught about unconditional love.
Unconditional love is not a desiring kind of love or the love between lovers. Instead, it is the highest attainable mind-set and understanding towards oneself and the whole universe. Whoever is in harmony, deep peace and deep faith, uses willpower (1) constructively (e.g. prayers), lives a simple life (2), does not judge (3), has no fear (4), is creative (5), loves himself (6), is full of charity (7), has escaped the cycle of re-incarnation (8), is wise (9), self-realised (10), connected with the universe (11) and connected with the divine consciousness (12).

The seven deadly sins suggest that every human is a sinner. Pride, envy, gluttony, lust, anger, greed and sloth are indeed unbalanced mindsets that increase karma and pain. In this respect, the concept of deadly sins is useful, but it is also harmful because nobody is a sinner. The concept of sin is a kind of masochism in the strict psychological sense, and this is deeply rooted in the human consciousness. To punish oneself leads to the punishment of others for their hypothetical sins: this is sadism.
Masochism and sadism are dangerous psychological concepts (3) which can even increase karma. Instead, we need to forgive ourselves and other people. This is another important message from Jesus and the Bible.

Prayers are a useful technique to find a way to God and to achieve something. Prayers are based on focused will (1) and its creative power. By focusing this willpower on a worthwhile goal (God, healthiness, love etc.), a limited creative impulse gets sent out to the universe and slightly improves the universe.

Buddha

Before his enlightenment (10), Buddha was fascinated by the nature of suffering. He eventually found out that (psychological) suffering is real but can be dissolved. Physical pain, however, is inevitable. Initially, Buddha started his practice as an ascetic, which was usual at that time. He then realised that extremes of that kind should be avoided instead.

Every aspect of the 12 Fields is relevant and none should be suppressed. However, whoever lives like an ascetic retracts himself from society (7), possesses nothing (2), neglects his body (6) and suppresses his desires (5).
This approach can be beneficial in individual cases but is not a generally valid concept for evolution.

Instead, Buddha taught the eightfold path after attaining self-realisation (10):

Right View (9)
Right Resolve (3)
Right Speech (3)
Right Conduct (5, 6, 7)
Right Livelihood (2, 6)
Right Effort (1, 10)
Right Mindfulness (4, 5, 6)
Right Samadhi (1)

The eightfold path tries to balance all aspects of life and to avoid further karmic involvement (8).

Until today, an interesting form of meditation is practised by Buddhists. This technique is supported by the repetition of mantras, similar to the meditation techniques in Yoga. The practitioner concentrates on breathing. Breathing is related to the mind because it is related to the heart chakra. Whenever we focus our attention on the heart chakra or on our breathing, the heart chakra opens slightly and the mind comes to rest.
Therefore, this technique promotes a calm mind, insights into the truth and increases wisdom (9).
The Buddhist approach to overcoming karma has the advantage of proper and flawless documentation, which

minimises the risk of manipulation by man. It is especially positive that Buddhism offers a philosophy and techniques unobtrusively, without any sense of superiority or lust for power.

Even though Buddha was one of the most valuable spiritual teachers in this world, this does not mean that all people should become Buddhists, or even monks, to escape the cycle of re-incarnation (8). We may and should live and enjoy all aspects of life moderately. This includes sexuality and other pleasures.

For those deciding to spend their lives in temples of their chosen religion, this may be beneficial and in accordance with their karmic needs and/or evolutionary intents, but it does not mean that they live a better life or that they are spiritually more advanced.
In many cases, people feel attracted by temples and religions because they subconsciously remember this from past lives. Maybe they miss these things. And in those cases, it can even be more challenging and more beneficial to master the earthly life, which is full of social and cultural challenges, instead.

The Original (Ancient) Tantra

Tantra is an ancient science and spiritual practice whose original rituals are not documented and therefore lost to a huge extent. Modern Tantra seminars are increasing in popularity but they are comparatively less spiritual and less pure.

'Shiva-Shakti' is the underlying Hindu philosophy in which the idea of the 12 Fields can easily be found on a higher level:

According to 'Shiva-Shakti,' Shiva is God in its passive state (12), containing infinite potential. As soon as a dynamic arises, God gets into motion. This is Shakti and can be found in the Fields (1-11) in various intensities. The philosophy suggests that the Kundalini force (Shakti) is situated and stored at the lower end of the spine (6). If activated, this energy rises upwards along the spine (axis (6)-(12)) to unite with the crown chakra (12). This leads to an energetic explosion within the Yogi that might - in the best case - lead to enlightenment i.e. to overcoming the cycle of re-incarnation (8).

Sexual practice is strongly related to the sacral chakra, which is connected to the third eye. An activation of the sacral chakra can therefore activate the third eye and its aspects.

There is no hierarchy between Shiva and Shakti. Instead, they describe the two principle states of infinity. Their coexistence and the oscillation between separation and unity is symbolised in Hinduism as a divine dance.

Around the time of Krishna, Tantra was a highly spiritual and common practice in today's Indian region. Spiritually advanced children were carefully chosen by tantric monks (comparable to selecting the next Dalai Lama in Tibetic Buddhism) and then integrated in the highly protected temple life in order to become sexualised and spiritualised by their presence and later by participation in tantric practices.

Since this process can lead to very high energetic and spiritual states, it was vital to apply purifying rituals in order to attain pure and God-seeking thoughts and to purify the body. Temple life was only dedicated to realising God. Sexuality was not practised for sensual pleasure but purely to achieve spiritual goals.
Those practitioners, eventually attaining a mastership in Tantra, had a very strong energetic field (aura) thanks to their open and purified chakras. Consequently, these monks had supernatural powers. In principle, Tantra was a valid means to achieve enlightenment.

Tantra, at that time, was a pure, spiritual practice but potentially risky in practice. Energetic accidents frequently occurred whereby highly energised sacral chakra collapsed or reversed their polarity. Some practitioners became proud and a few were even killed by suspicious crowds.

As a result of such accidents and the increasing cultural tabooing of sexuality, Tantra slowly disappeared in favour of other yoga techniques such as meditation. Due to the lacking documentation about the exact rituals and processes, today's Tantra seminars only focus on the discovery of sexuality and the resolution of blockades. In some seminars, there are even attempts to achieve this with strangers who sometimes have questionable intents. Currently, Tantra is not a technique which is sufficient to achieve enlightenment.

Yoga / Hinduism

Hinduism and Yoga are very closely related. In the western world, it is erroneously assumed that Yogis believe in many Gods. In fact, those Gods and Goddesses symbolise aspects of infinity, just how every person fulfills different roles in daily life: as a partner, friend, colleague, child, parent etc. I am all of these things, but I behave differently in these roles according to the requirements and circumstances involved.

Yoga and Hinduism assume one single God which cannot be described and which is infinite. This God is called 'Brahman' (12).
Whenever God gets into motion, it has three functions as the creator 'Brahma' (1 to 5), 'Rudra-Shiva' (7 to 11), who transforms creation back to its origin, and Vishnu, which is love and wisdom on the axis (3, 9) that holds everything together.

In Hinduism, Brahma does not get worshipped. There is only one temple in India dedicated to Brahma. Since Brahma is, like anything else, a divine aspect, the lack of worship seems surprising. Yet Brahma has fulfilled his task of creating the universe. No matter whether one lives an earthly or spiritual (which is in fact both spiritual) life, mankind is on its way back to its origin, and Shiva, who transforms and educates us, is responsible for this path. This is what gives us a better understanding of why Hindus ask Shiva, instead of Brahma, for guidance and support.

The spiritual path of Bhakti-Yoga is mainly practised in India. Devotional rituals are applied to worship God. This

could be done by singing mantras or performing rituals such as 'pujas.'
Such techniques increase the devotion of the practitioner and create a high and perceivable energy field.
Strictly speaking, devotion for the divine is absurd because we and everything else is God.

Through this technique, the practitioner does not only symbolically lay in the dust before God, but also literally and physically. Some people think 'God is everything, I am nothing.' This creates an inseparable gap between God and mankind.
This approach is beneficial whenever an ego is lacking devotion and humility. In fact, spirituality is always a reminder of our true yet forgotten identity. The will (1), thinking (3), feeling (4) and desiring (5) are focused on the divine in order to get rid of karma and to avoid new karma being collected.

Karma Yoga is similar. In this discipline, people work selflessly for a good cause by not expecting gratitude or reward. This also increases devotion. Karma Yoga is not about completing a task efficiently. Instead, it is about keeping the right attitude during any activity by dedicating the activity to God.

Meditation (Raja Yoga) is for good reason the most commonly applied technique by Yogis for promoting self-realisation. Of course, reaching the highest step requires, like in all other spiritual techniques, the soul to have nearly completed the cycle of re-incarnation. There are only a few karmic issues and evolutionary lessons left over.

The most efficient meditation technique is mantra meditation, in which a mantra such as 'Om' or 'Om namah Shivay' is repeatedly recited while focusing one's attention, for example, on the third eye or heart chakra.

The will (1) becomes focused on the divine (12). The body (6) comes to rest. The surrounding environment (2) is not noticed. The thinking mind (3) is calmed down and gets purified. This calms down the upcoming emotions (4) and desires (5).
The mantra, as such, contains a high frequency energy (12) that fills up our mind (3, 9) instead of the usual thoughts.

Perceptive people can see how light enters the crown chakra (12) during meditation in a spiraled way and then spreads in the energetic system. Hence, by meditating, we establish a connection with the divine state (12), purify our mind, open the third eye (2, 11) and/or the heart chakra (3, 9) and avoid negative thoughts, passions and new karma.
This is why meditation is such a common and powerful technique: it promotes the fields that transform us and calms down the fields that further bind us to the objects of the world.

Hatha-Yoga is gaining in popularity. In the western hemisphere, Yoga is erroneously mistaken as Hatha-Yoga, which is mainly composed of conscious physical movements, breathing techniques and relaxations. The original Yoga philosophy is not a spiritual technique that could lead to enlightenment. It is just a technique that helps the Yogi remain physically fit and flexible while practicing the spiritual Yoga disciplines mentioned above and below. Meditating for hours can be stressful and painful for the body; this is why some Yogis apply the gymnastics of Hatha-Yoga.

Kundalini Yoga is similar to Hatha Yoga but it is much more energetic and intense. It can therefore achieve results such as the Kundalini (Shakti) at the bottom of the spine (6) rises along the spine (axis (6) - (12)) to unite with Shiva in the crown chakra (12). Depending on the attained level of spiritual advancement, this technique can lead to supernatural powers (by opening the chakras) or even to enlightenment.

Jnana Yoga is the Yoga of wisdom. It tries to reach enlightenment through a more cognitive approach in order to understand the true nature of existence and creation. This is often done by studying philosophical concepts of Vedanta. However, this Yoga path is supposed to be the most difficult one. Not many Yogis have reached the highest spiritual levels through Jnana Yoga.
The modern Vedanta teacher, Ramesh Balsekar, wrote books until his recent death, reminding the reader of the idea behind Buddhism and Yoga and that the individual human being is not the doer of any action. In fact, countless actions happen each moment in the universe but in reality, it is God (1-12) that is acting. Consequently, this leads to the concept that there is absolutely no reason to feel guilty, ashamed, hateful etc.
We, as apparent human beings, can leave it all to God.

Other lines of Jnana Yoga let the practitioner meditate over the question 'Who am I?' This approach aims to negate everything perceivable ('I am not that') and to be, in fact, the indescribable principle that remains. This can create a moment in consciousness where the Yogi does not only think to be God in essence but where the Yogi deeply realises it forever.

Simplicity - Truth - Love

About 40 years ago in India, the spiritual teacher, Babaji, taught that one should live a life in simplicity, love and truth in order to achieve self-realisation.
This approach nicely covers the circle of the 12 Fields.
On the left side, around Field (12), there is the highest truth, namely our true origin and our temporarily forgotten identity.
In our heart and mind (3, 9), we should keep and increase love. On the physical level, around field (6), we should live a simple life. Not 'simple' in the sense of poverty, but in the sense of living a moderate life in which we do not unnecessarily further complicate karmic involvement.
All aspects of life may and should be lived but always moderately and by remembering our true identity. According to the cosmic laws, all other actions will lead to a corrective measure, which means karma.

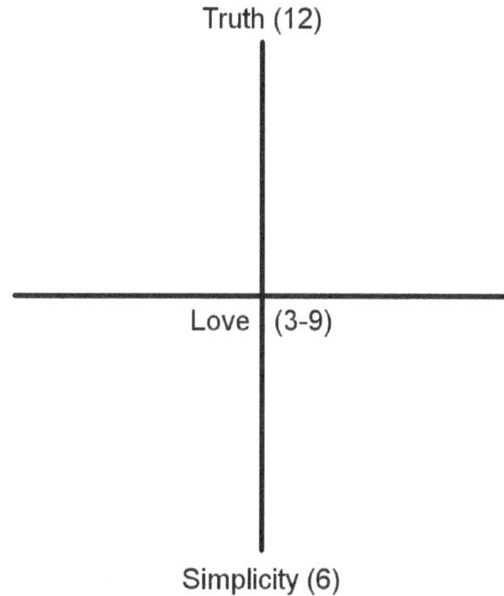

Image 6: The backbone of the 12 Fields as love, simplicity and truth

Past Life Regression

During a past life regression, a client is steadily guided by a therapist into a deep relaxation. In this state, past life memories of life-between-lives memories can appear from the subconscious.
Typically, the client and the therapist are guided by their invisible spirits to a relevant traumatic memory which still has a negative effect on the client's emotional body.
In order to minimise this impact, it can be beneficial to look at the memory again and to come to better

conclusions such as acceptance, love, farewell and forgiveness.
This purifies the subconscious and heals the client accordingly.
In practice, this technique is also useful to positively break down the cognitive view of the world (3) of the client by experiencing that their past lives are real. Clients can then start to build up a more holistic view of the world (9).

Shamanism

In Shamanism, the thinking mind (3) is purposely irritated and calmed down by rhythmic drumming. Similarly to a past life regression, this moment of inner silence can be used to get in touch with the spiritual realm. There, we can meet and perceive spirits of many kinds that will give us guidance, healing and advice. Alternatively, we can use the moment of cognitive relaxation to look at past life memories, as done during a regression.
Therefore, the effect of Shamanism is comparable to a regression: we can contribute to healing and breaking down the cognitive view of the world in favour of a holistic view. The subtle world can become an increasingly important part of our lives by integrating Shamanism into it.

Karmic and Chakra Astrology

As mentioned in the first chapters, it is not a coincidence that the 12 Fields correspond to the 12 houses in astrology. Apparently, the universe has been designed by Brahma in (1) such that underlying principles can be found in the macrocosm and microcosm.
In theory, the universe could have been programmed such that these principles cannot be found anywhere and the moment of birth could not be decoded in any way.

Thanks to the pioneer work of Jeff Green, the karmic analysis of the birth-chart leads to a deep insight into the motives for this incarnation and into past life memories (Pluto & south node), old traumata (Saturn, maybe Chiron) and life-tasks (Pluto's polarity point, north node).
Interestingly, the astrologic analysis leads to the same results as a past life regression. The difference lays only in the level of detail. The birth-chart cannot provide detailed information about the life conditions during a past life (country, age, climate, gender, etc.) but it describes the principle behind that life. On the other hand, astrology is easier to apply.

Provided somebody learns everything about his karma and evolutionary intents, this neither resolves any karma nor frees it from the cycle of re-incarnation. Yet this knowledge is very valuable because it promotes a holistic view of the world, promotes acceptance of one's life conditions / limitations and helps to use one's energy more constructively and in a more focused way. All in all, this makes the learning process on earth more efficient and avoids further karmic involvement to a certain degree.

Presumably, how far a soul is spiritually advanced could one day be derived from the birth-chart. At the moment, this is impossible. There are a few concepts in literature and on the internet, but these fail in practice, which is maybe a good thing for the time being.

In a similar way, there are many theories about the chakra system within the birth-chart. Maybe the understanding and application of the cycle of the 12 Fields can show how the functioning, traumas and blockades of the chakra system can be derived astrologically. From my point of view, the analysis of the corresponding houses and signs leads to very useful results and can, combined with the karmic astrology, also show why a chakra functions the way it does.

Example: The functioning of the sacral chakra can be derived by analysing house 5, house 7, Libra and Leo.

5. Conclusions / Perspective

The understanding of the Fields in the universe and in the human being is very beneficial.

All 12 Fields are states of the same God. There is God in rest, God in motion, God involved in matter, God in confusion and the liberated God. It is always God that acts; through every soul and every being.
That's why the spiritual question of where God can be found and how to reach God does not make sense, because there is nothing but God.
However, as a result of a dynamic process, this one God has initiated a movement where apparent individuals that have temporarily forgotten their origin live in confusion, and due to their inherent willpower, even their karmic involvement to matter increases.

For us on earth, the 12 Fields request us to do two things:

1) We should be full of love and peace
2) We should go through a transformation to become liberated from the cycle of re-incarnation

'Love yourself but please change.' This may initially seem contradictory: why should I accept myself while there is a need to become somebody else?
Some spiritual teachers even suggest that everybody destroy their ego. However, this could be seen as having many flaws; surely it is anyway not in man's nature to partially destroy himself.

In fact, without the ego that was created during the Fields (1) to (6), interpersonal relationships and the corresponding learning experiences would not even be possible. The ego should not be demonised.
Love means acceptance and harmony. By loving ourselves and the divine, we accept the cycle of the 12 Fields and we realise that it is God who acts and who was involved in creation for whatever reason. That is why we may, and should, accept and respect ourselves and each other, although there is work to be done on getting rid of erroneous identification.

Actually, everything that ever existed, currently exists or in future will exist is of divine origin and divine nature. There cannot be anything beyond infinity. Therefore, there is only one correct form of identification, namely the one with infinity itself. All other possible identifications must inevitably be mistakes.
Such a mistake is not catastrophic, but thanks to the remaining limited creative power of the incarnated soul, the mistake is deepened and becomes the foundation of wrong conclusions and corresponding actions. Karma adds up to the sum of all unbalanced actions and inexperienced intentions. The worst and most brutal things that human beings ever did can be traced back to this initial misidentification. The concept of karma is very real but whose karma is it? Again, strictly speaking, it is God's karma. Karma is cosmically accumulated.

In practice, the concept of incarnating souls which have and resolve karma is a helpful model. Yet this model is a simplification and therefore not completely correct.
Strictly speaking, there are no individual souls. If, for example, a soul has a certain evolutionary intent to learn

creativity during an incarnation, it takes a suitable quality and quantity of karma from the universal karma and goes down to earth. Maybe, this soul takes karma such that the creativity is initially blocked. And through this experience, it starts to reflect deeply and constrictively over creativity. During a past life regression therapy, this soul would be able to see memory fragments about (maybe several) past lives that caused the blockade. However, strictly speaking, this was not necessarily the same soul. Whatever the memories are, the story told once indeed happened, but it happened to the one being that we all are.

In order to remain pragmatic and less philosophical, it is, in practice, valid and useful to assume individual souls and individual karma. And since God, in the shape of humans, experiences pain on earth and is confused by its identity, the question is how to overcome the cycle of re-incarnation efficiently in the sense of speed and with as little pain as possible. In other words: how can we reach a high degree of consciousness and unconditional love in the most efficient way?

To achieve this, our society and each individual require a clean spiritual framework in order to give us an idea from childhood about our existence and the identity of God.
Ideally, there will be one nameless science dealing with the universe in the far future which includes and aligns today's knowledge from sciences, psychology, medical science and spirituality. This knowledge can then be increased and corrected steadily and carefully through responsible institutions and boards.
An appropriate spiritual framework is voluntary, en-lightening and never thinks in terms of sin and atonement.

Such a framework must neither bind people compulsively nor scare them. Instead, it informs people that they are of divine origin, which even includes their karma and their imperfections. This spiritual framework will never claim to be complete. It will not spread by force but will evolve with mankind. This rather scientific spiritual approach includes spiritual and educational practices that can be helpful in resolving karma and increasing our understanding of unconditional love. Consequently, the spiritual framework results in giving a direction to all political, social, psychological, spiritual and personal aspects of life.

There have always been spiritually advanced civilisations in human history. In such civilisations, an exchange with the spiritual realm was intensively established and socially accepted, for example in the early Old Egypt, the native Indians in North-America, their Siberian ancestors, Yogis, the first Christians and the early civilisations in Central-America.

Today, this exchange with the spiritual realm is atrophied and not socially accepted, but it should be re-established intensively in order to co-operate with spiritual beings closely to thus improve mankind.

The chakras of many people are very open so that they can easily establish a good connection with the spiritual realm. Instead of declaring the limited insights of science (3) as the highest truth, we need both science and the connection with the spiritual world through intuition and the higher chakras.

Everybody on earth has a body (6), interpersonal relationships (7) and is bound by karma and an evolutionary intent to the cycle of re-incarnation (8).

Through the course of all incarnations, the souls becomes wiser (9) while still desiring sensual pleasures (5). During this predominantly painful journey, the urge to escape the cycle of re-incarnation increases. These souls call themselves 'spiritual seekers.' They then try out religions, philosophies and spiritual practices, but every soul that simply lives its life according to its likes and dislikes is fully spiritual. Many, however, are simply not aware of this.

A soul has escaped the cycle of re-incarnation when it transits from Field (9) to Field (10). Then, love (9) is fully developed and the soul realises for the first time (10) to be God itself. The soul does not only remember its identity; it also recaps knowledge and capabilities attained during the process of going through the Fields.

How can a soul get to this desirable state? The simplest and most legitimate way would be to re-incarnate patiently and to co-operate with the guidance from the spiritual realm. Then, the cycle will one day reach its natural end by achieving the ability to love and by gaining wisdom. No soul will ever be forgotten. Every soul will one day definitely reach this point and nobody should listen to religions which claim to be vital for achieving such goals. This point of view is man-made.

To many spiritual seekers, this theoretic and relaxed approach is not enough. They are tired of being humans and want to accelerate the process. It then makes sense to study spiritual philosophies and to try out various spiritual techniques.
Enlightenment of any kind requires the experience of many interpersonal relationships and the resolving of many karmic issues. This highly complex process takes

many thousands of years in total. Depending on the level of advancement, spiritual practice can simplify the process, but only to a certain extent.

Nevertheless, good spiritual techniques are not a waste of time for they valuably contribute to shortening the cycle of re-incarnation by making it less painful. There are less detours and tangents. And who actually knows if enlightenment is close or if spiritual efforts are just an intermezzo on a long journey? Nearly nobody does.

In general, the desired Fields (9) to (12) can be reached by avoiding further involvement and by increasing one's wisdom:

Not to get involved means to live the aspects of the Fields (1) to (6) attentively and moderately:

> Field (1, 7): A conscious use of willpower (also regarding the conduct of interpersonal relationships and social attitudes).
>
> Field (2, 8): A moderate relation to matter and finances. Life may, and should, be enjoyed, but this joy is not the meaning of life.
>
> Field (3): The conscious avoiding of negative and judgmental thoughts.
>
> Field (4): The conscious avoiding of negative emotions.
>
> Field (5): A moderate integration of sensual pleasures and passion.

Field (6): An uncomplicated and simple way of living in order to keep the body and energetic system healthy.

At the same time, we need to get rid of legacy (karma), purify ourselves and long for evolution. This reduces the existing involvement into matter:

Field (1, 2): A clean spiritual framework and, for example, the subsequent practising of prayers focuses the individual intents (1) more strongly onto the divine (12).

Field (3): By studying appropriate spiritual philosophies (e.g. Vedanta, Buddhism, etc.) and by meditating over the true nature of the universe, intellect - being the little brother of wisdom - contributes to the increase of wisdom.

Meditation calms down the cognitive mind (3) and opens the mind via the crown chakra (12) for higher energies. Reciting mantras can then further purify and increase the energetic level of the soul.

Field (4): The subconscious gets purified by overcoming negative emotions (desire, sadness, fear). For example, in Buddhism this is achieved by focusing the attention on one's thoughts (3) and feelings (4).

Field (5): By the hypothetical application of the ancient Tantra, whose detailed processes got lost, the re-union of Shiva (12) and Shakti (6) could be achieved.

Field (6): Chakras could be opened by the awakening of the kundalini force at the lower end of the spine, e.g. through kundalini yoga.
In addition, the physical body and the energetic system could be purified by ayurveda, homeopathy, acupuncture, Reiki, therapeutic fasting and a healthy diet. The subconscious would benefit from this as well.

Field (7, 8): By understanding and accepting the involvement into the cycle of re-incarnation (8), karmic issues can be resolved and the evolution of the soul can continue smoothly. On an interpersonal level, this process can be accelerated by charitable acts, forgiving ourselves and forgiving others based on the understanding of our unity, inter-connection and infinity.

It is definitely not necessary (and sometimes even counter-productive) to join a religion or at least to apply the rules of a religion without questioning it.
The philosophic core of a religion originates mostly - but not always - from the teachings of a highly advanced soul that was purposely incarnated to live and teach to love by example.
In some cases, the origin of a religion or sect is purely human and manipulative. It requires an immense clarity and ability to discriminate in order to separate en-lightening teachings from the dark ones.

Many precious teachings of highly advanced souls have been turned into constructs like religions by imperfect humans. This is why religions combine light and shadow at the same time; light in terms of the more or less falsified teachings and shadow through misinterpretation, abuse of power and elitism.
Therefore, the combination of light and shadow is simultaneously precious and unskillful. This gives room for much improvement.

Any religious concept that feels superior and even actively fights other concepts acts against the universal principle of love and unity. What it does instead is bind supporters to their man-made structures. This cannot be helpful and presumably is not in the spirit of the underlying teachings if it were ever to have originated from a highly advanced soul.

Either these highly advanced souls could successfully realise their true self or they are beings that were never meant to be part of the cycle of re-incarnation but still decided to become a human in order to complete a certain task.
In India, the term 'Avatar' is being increasingly used for the latter beings. Believers assume that it is God itself (12) who incarnates. I find this contradictory since God in its state (12) is passive and without shape. The highest perceivable beings must still be in (11). These beings have almost infinite powers and are connected with the universe, but their powers are still limited and not without attributes as in (12).

The spiritual seeker should be very careful with people showing supernatural powers. Many wise souls gain these

powers as a kind of side-effect of their spiritual level. However, there are also confused and less advanced souls that may have acquired certain powers for karmic reasons.
Supernatural powers are not a sign of enlightenment, and compared with the omnipotence of (12), these supernatural powers such as clairvoyance or materialisation are simply nothing.
The undemonstrative example of living, praying and showing love is a better indication of a precious source of inspiration.

So, how should we deal with religions? Extreme views are always wrong. It is advisable to study teachings and philosophies with an open and critical mind. Those teachings should be considered and checked for validity. Following a religion can be a useful experience to integrate oneself socially, to be charitable and to discuss spiritual matters in a community. Yet such a step that could be correct on individual and karmic levels, in general, not required. The main thing is to find valuable teachings for oneself that somehow increase the ability to love unconditionally, be wise and increase one's deeper understanding of life.

Based on a hopefully pure and enlightening spiritual framework, we could better understand that we are all one and should subsequently live a simple, loving and truth-seeking life.

Compared with the currently high degree of confusion of mankind, an appropriate spiritual framework would be a huge evolutionary step that could lead to a balanced and conscious relationship with ourselves, fellow human beings, the environment, the whole planet and the surrounding spiritual realm. This will fundamentally lead to harmony with everything.

The 'unconditional love' which was already discussed in the sense of harmony, acceptance and unity, is the highest principle of life:

Harmony with ourselves (6) leads to a holistic and preventive medical system, to healthy agriculture / food and to personal self-fulfillment at work.

A conscious and loving relationship with fellow human beings (7) leads to true humanity, empathy, social politics and co-operation instead of competition.

Love for the world fundamentally leads to environmental protection and technological progress. It also establishes a connection with the surrounding spiritual world to which we will return anyway after our physical death.

Love for God leads to a spiritual and philosophical reflection about the universe and our origin and identity within it.

What does this mean for today's society in a democratic, western and wealthy country?

Capitalism and competition are evolutions that emphasise greed, exploitation and conflict. This massively contradicts the principle of love. Instead, moderate and loving values such as integrity, empathy and co-operation should be taught from childhood onwards. This would be the expression of an uncomplicated life in love.

Sensual pleasures and technological progress are achievements of capitalism that should remain a part of our lives. We may, and should, enjoy life and there is nothing wrong with making life easier by using technology, but these aspects should not be the first objective or priority of any society.

Goods should first of all comply with ethic criteria so that, for example, the disposal of unhealthy or pollutant substances can be reduced by appropriate standards and their supervision.

Small children and young people are very open, perceptive and thirsty for knowledge. This is why they need parental love, especially at the beginning as this is important for a later stepwise transition into an educational system consisting of highly skilled teachers.
Whilst learning at school, children should not be being prepared for competitions but should instead be being made aware of the spiritual framework that explains the need for co-operation and that supports them in finding their true talents and evolutionary tasks, encouraging them to live a psychologically and physically healthy life.

To protect and improve this system, the steady growth of society should be supported by educational and political measures in order to attain a higher degree of spiritual, political and social education among people.

Man's negative influence on the environment should be reduced for obvious self-preserving and moral reasons. This could, for example, be achieved by a steady reduction of pollutant substances and the introduction of ecological agriculture.

A physically, mentally and emotionally healthy person is the pre-requisite for a satisfied life, harmonic inter-personal relationships and intuitive knowledge.

The achievements of medical science such as diagnostics, emergency medicine and operation techniques should be further researched and optimised. For the causal healing of diseases, alternative methods (such as homeopathy, acupuncture, meditation, etc.) should be further researched and integrated step by step, according to their maturity. This includes the promotion of mental health and the increase of inner peace.

From childhood onwards, we should be taught how to deal with our thoughts and emotions. There are already enough useful concepts and techniques to achieve this, and this will clearly reduce the physical and emotional pain that people often go through.

Many cognitive concepts and beliefs are hardly worth continuing. Instead, we should start to understand from childhood onwards that we are of divine origin, but because and despite of that, we need to be careful about how we apply our willpower, thoughts and feelings so that we do not become unnecessarily further involved in creation.

Such a spiritual framework will not only help the individual, but also the countries and mankind as such. Man-made concepts such as war, imperialism, competition, terrorism, nationalism and genocide will then appear to us as absurd and insane as they are.

Ultimately, mankind is one being that became involved in this planet. Karma also arose and many fatal social decisions and actions of the past are still not resolved from a karmic point of view. If this happens one day, and it definitely will, life on earth will be at its peak on an individual and social level like never before. Maybe then, when the divine, in its dynamic form, will be involved in creation whilst being full of understanding and love, will the benefit of incarnation become more obvious to 'us'.

Zeitfracht Medien GmbH
Ferdinand-Jühlke-Straße 7
99095 Erfurt, Deutschland
produktsicherheit@kolibri360.de